pueblo and this shirt would be worn at the many religious ceremonies that regulated their lives.

She sat beside him in the late afternoon sun watching the younger children play on the pueblo rooftops. Even in July the cave was cool. It had been carefully chosen so the morning sun warmed it in the winter and shade protected them from the blistering summer sun.

Times were good in the Tonto Basin, but her people's stories told of cycles of rain and plentiful harvests followed by drought and hardship. A precarious life balanced against the natural world.

WATER CARVES A HOME. More than a billion years before this mythical Salado woman gazed over the Salt River all of central Arizona lay buried beneath a shallow sea. Over the millennia, layer upon layer of siltstone, sandstone, mudstone and limestone were deposited on the tidal flats and in the shallow marine environment of the western continental shelf. This thick layer of Precambrian sediment, known as the Apache Group, formed the rocks now exposed in the great cliffs that tower above the Salt River.

Then followed millions of years during which the geologic record for this part of Arizona is incomplete. Geologists theorize that the sea encroached many times upon the land, depositing thousands of feet of sediment, then retreated, allowing the forces of erosion to erase the work of the sea. These cycles of deposition and erosion repeated themselves many times during the Paleozoic and early Mesozoic Eras, between 600 and 100 million years ago.

During the late Mesozoic and early Cenozoic Eras, between fifty and 100 million years ago, tremendous forces wrenched at the land. The plates of the earth's crust relentlessly collided, thrusting huge blocks of rock upward into jagged, towering mountain ranges. Rocks were ripped apart, contorted, and masses of molten copper-bearing magma were forced into the cracks. Another cycle of erosion followed, wearing away the mountains and exposing deeply buried ore deposits and ancient rocks.

During the Mid-Tertiary Orogeny, fifteen to twenty-five million years ago, cataclismic volcanic activity formed the Superstition Mountains and other ranges in southern Arizona.

About eight to fifteen million years ago a final episode of deformation crudely defined the present topography of much of central Arizona. The Basin and Range Disturbance created vertical displacement along fault lines which lifted the major mountain ranges as basins collapsed between them. These basins then began to fill with rock debris washed down from the surrounding mountains. These sediments, known as the Gila Conglomerate, had accumulated to enormous depths, by the end of the Pleistocene, completely

filling the downfaulted basins. The bottom portion of this formation was then tightly cemented by minerals, such as calcium carbonate and silica, leached from ground water.

The forces of erosion finished sculpturing the Tonto Basin. Less than a million years ago, all of central Arizona was gently uplifted some 3 to 4 thousand feet. This uplift initiated a new cycle of erosion that continues today. Gradually, major stream systems developed which carried most of the Gila Conglomerate out of the Tonto Basin to the southwest. Only remnants of the firmly cemented lower edges of this formation can be seen today, in the plaster which coats the cliffs near the Tonto ruins.

Some 200,000 years ago water began to fashion caves in the ancient Apache Group sediments. These shattered seabed sediments appeared as cliff forming strata that eventually sheltered Salado homes. The Apache Group is composed of several distinct sedimentary layers, but the one that most affected the lives of the Salado is a 600 foot thick layer of firmly cemented sandstone, quartzite, claystone and siltstone, known to geologists as the Dripping Spring Quartzite.

In the upper section of the Dripping Spring Quartzite lies a fifty to seventy-five foot thick band of thinly laminated, closely jointed siltstone that is especially susceptible to the weathering process known as spalling. Spalling—the breaking off of thin layers of rock—began as water dissolved the cementing minerals which bound together the grains of sand and silt. Continued cycles of freezing and thawing enlarged cracks in the rock until pieces tumbled onto the floor of the cave. Small stalactites and thin layers of flowstone on the cave walls show where groundwater has moved through the rock over thousands of years as this natural process continues to enlarge the caves.

Seven hundred years ago, when the Salado came seeking a protected place to live, they found natural caves sufficiently large to house a small community, littered with all the building stone they required.

THE LAND BETWEEN. The Salt River rises in the White Mountains to the east, forces its way through the steep-walled Salt River Canyon, and finally emerges from its confinement onto the wide flood plain of the Tonto Basin. This large intermontane basin is located in the transition zone between the high mesas and deep canyons of the Colorado Plateau region to the north and the deserts of the Basin and Range Province to the south. Physiographical and biological overlapping create a meeting ground for plant communities where many desert species reach their northernmost tolerance and northern species their southernmost extension.

The broad valley floor and steeply sloping surrounding mountains contained a variety of microenvironments that produced a wide range of resources within a small geographic area. The river valley, once covered with rich alluvial soils, produced good crops when water was applied to the fields. Thick stands of mesquite, walnut, and sycamore trees grew along water courses and near springs. Saguaro, cholla, prickly pear, jojoba, and other species that produce edible buds and fruits grew on the steeper slopes and mesas. At higher elevations, the pinyon-juniper belt was rich in game and produced other varieties of edible fruits and nuts.

The area was a natural contact zone between several major prehistoric Southwestern cultures. The Anasazi from the Four Corners area of Utah, Arizona, New Mexico and Colorado; the Mogollon of the mountains of southeastern Arizona and southwestern New Mexico; and the Hohokam of the river valleys and deserts of southern Arizona may all have found familiar environments to exploit within this basin. The Salado culture, which developed here around 1150, is probably the result of interactions and cultural exchanges among these groups.

ENTER: EARLY MAN. Exactly when nomadic people first wandered into the Tonto Basin may never be known. As early as 10,000 B.C. Paleo-Indians may have traveled in seasonal patterns throughout the Southwest hunting the mammoth and other extinct mammals and gathering wild grasses and seeds.

The Tonto Basin has yet to yield

Gila monster and granite.

evidence of human occupation before the Middle Archaic period (5000–1000 B.C.). However, it is difficult to believe that the diversity of wild plant species and game attracted by the permanently flowing Salt River would not have enticed man here on a seasonal basis long before this time. The ephemeral nature of the tools and hearths of these early hunters and gatherers make their campsites difficult to locate. Evidence of these groups who made no pottery, may be deeply buried by later sedimentary deposits, or perhaps such sites were destroyed by later occupation of the area.

The first permanent occupation of the Tonto Basin by sedentary agricultural people occurred between A.D. 700 and 800. Sites from this period have led some archeologists to suggest that the indigenous (possible Archaic) population was assimilated by colonists from the Hohokam culture who were then moving in from the lower Gila and Salt River valleys.

These desert farmers depended upon a constant supply of water to grow their irrigated crops of corn, squash, beans and cotton. An extensive system of canals diverted water from the river banks to their fields. The Colonial era (A.D. 550–900) was a time of population growth and rapid expansion for the Hohokam culture. As these farmers sought new areas to colonize, they naturally looked for landscapes which were compatible with their current life-style. The fertile bottom lands of the upper Salt River were a perfect choice.

By A.D. 850 the Hohokam occupation of the Tonto Basin was well established. Small villages of up to a dozen pithouse structures lined the edges of the flood plain. These houses were constructed within excavated pits, with wood and brush walls.

The Hohokam continued to inhabit the basin for the next 300 years, farming the alluvial terraces and sending work parties into the foothills to gather wild foods and to hunt game. Unfortunately, data from the early Hohokam occupation of the basin is scarce, due to the inundation of much of the area by Roosevelt Lake in 1911.

THE SALADO EMERGE. By A.D. 1150, small farming villages were strung along the edge of the flood plain from one end of the basin to the other. These village sites show us a culture in transition; pottery types, burial practices, house structures, and settlement patterns appear that can no longer be considered pure Hohokam.

In the late 1920s, pioneering archeologist Harold Gladwin identified these new cultural characteristics, calling the people who created them "Salado," meaning "salty." The name was chosen for the Río Salado, or Salt River, which brought life to their homeland.

Gladwin believed this new development was created by migrations of people from the upper Little Colorado River area into the Tonto Basin. He suggested that these groups brought most of the characteristically Salado traits with them from the north.

This theory of Salado migration has been questioned by later archeologists. Other explanations of Salado origins have been proposed, including migrations from other pueblo cultures to the north and east. Newer evidence suggests that the Salado tradition may not, for the most part, be the result of actual invasion from the north, but simply a regional variation of the Hohokam tradition which had been established in the basin 400 years earlier. Many of the early Salado sites were constructed atop Colonial period Hohokam sites, and there are many similarities between the artifacts, architecture, and settlement patterns of the two cultures. The differences between the Hohokam in the Phoenix area and the Salado in the Tonto Basin may have developed primarily because of differences in local environment, in local raw materials, and from contact with non-Hohokam populations—primarily Mogollon groups to the north and east.

The Tonto Basin was a natural travel corridor and may have provided a primary trade route between the plateau people to the north and the desert dwellers to the south. Certainly Salado architecture, ceramics, and other cultural materials show influences from all of the surrounding cultures.

Regardless of their origins, a well-established Salado culture existed in the Tonto Basin by A.D. 1200. These early Salado settlements were regularly spaced along the river valleys close to their irrigable fields. During the Salado era, the Salt River Valley was a broad, flat, almost marshy area where water flowed through cattails, river reeds, and grasses for most of the year.

When irrigation canals were dug to the river, water flowed freely onto the fields of corn, squash, beans, and amaranth. These canals were still visible on the flood plain until they were covered by the rising waters of Roosevelt Lake.

The typical Salado community

The Salt River as it may have appeared when the Salado lived here.

consisted of a multi-room masonry pueblo in which rooms shared adjacent walls. These communities were frequently enclosed within high compound walls, perhaps for protection or some unknown social function. Sites of 150 or more rooms have been recorded, though most pueblos have less than twenty rooms.

Dramatic population growth throughout this era is strongly indicated by the thousands of reported sites from all over the Salado area. As the population increased, the valley centers became crowded. Although most of the population remained in the valley and continued the major agricultural activities, around 1300 another segment of the population moved into higher elevations, possibly concentrating on non-agricultural activities. The cliff dwellings at Tonto National Monument were apparently built about this time. Perhaps these Salado became skilled craftsmen, and concentrated on hunting and gathering the native vegetation. These upland products could then have been traded in the valley, thus supplying the large towns with resources not locally available.

The Salado prospered in the Tonto Basin for approximately 300 years. They were a surprisingly healthy people. Skeletal remains have shown archeologists little evidence of the nutritional deficiencies so often found in puebloan agricultural societies. Although in many burials the teeth are worn down from the large amount of grit in their stone-ground food, the rate of dental decay was much lower than researchers expected.

Their population steadily increased, developing complex settlements and expanding their trade routes and influence into regions to the north and south. Macaw feathers found in Tonto ruin could only have come from Mesoamerica. The Salado developed specialized crafts and became increasingly dependent upon centralized leadership. Then, between 1400 and 1450, their culture collapsed and vanished from the Tonto Basin. What happened to the Salado has been a subject of debate for decades. Their departure seems to have been a part of the general abandonment of the southern mountains of the Southwest at about this time.

Gladwin suggested that the abandonment was due to Apache raiders, but recent findings have lead archeologists to conclude that the Apache were probably not in the area before A.D. 1500. Other causes, such as climatic change, salinization of croplands, and internal strife have been suggested, but the abandonment of the basin was probably the result of a number of complex factors.

Some archeologists suggest that the Salado may have moved north or west and been absorbed by the Hopi or Zuni cultures. Others believe they moved south into northern Mexico or into the lower Salt River Valley. These and other theories have yet to be proven. For now, the Salado

The Lower Ruin.

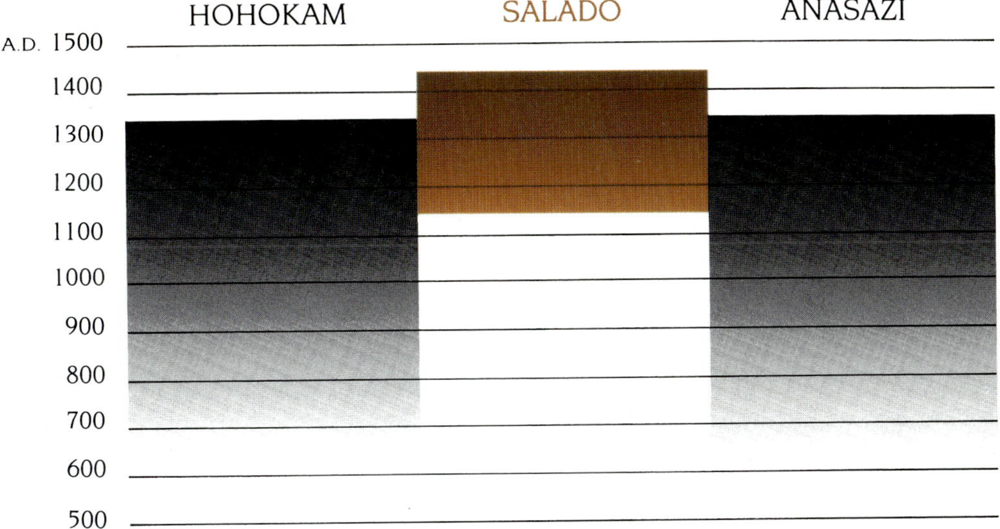

disappearance remains one of the fascinating mysteries of the prehistoric Southwest.

PRODUCE & THE DESERT'S BOUNTY. Although many modern visitors to the Southwest view the desert as a harsh and forbidding landscape, the Salado knew this sheltered valley could be a productive homeland. The diversity of both plant and animal species in the Tonto Basin, coupled with the Salado's intimate knowledge of their practical uses, turned these desert hillsides into a veritable supermarket of food, medicine, fiber and fashion.

The Salado lived close to the land, their lives intricately enmeshed with the annual cycles of rainfall and flooding that made agriculture possible in this arid land. The winter rainy season brings gentle soaking rains that penetrate the soil and nurture the lush growth of spring. In contrast, the summer monsoon season brings turbulent afternoon thunderstorms that could cause flash flooding, soil erosion, and crop damage. The climate of the Tonto Basin is mild and the growing season one of the longest in Arizona, lasting over 300 days. This fact alone made the area attractive to a farming people.

Corn was the single most important food and no other plant remains are so abundant in the archeological records of Salado sites. The introduction of this crop gradually eliminated the migratory foraging cycles of earlier hunting and gathering societies and provided stability and security to the Salado's sedentary life style. This important food source found its way into the American Southwest sometime around 2000 B.C. through the growing network of trade routes with southern Mexico. It became so important to the southwestern cultures that their reverence for this grain led to its use in religious ceremonies.

Corn could be prepared in a wide variety of ways. Hominy was made by soaking corn kernels in juniper ashes. When these kernels were boiled, the ashes and hulls washed off. If corn kernels were soaked and then parched in hot sand, the outer coat split, much like modern popcorn. Cornmeal, which was ground on stone slabs, could have been made into bread, griddlecakes, dumplings, or mush. And when the meal was completed, the corn cobs were dried and burned—an important benefit in an area with few other fuel sources.

The arrival of squash and beans, also from Mesoamerica, completed the triumvirate of Salado agricultural products. These early farmers soon discovered that crop yields were substantially increased when beans and corn were planted close together in the same field. Today we know that beans are legumes, plants whose root systems have the ability to replace the nitrogen which corn crops strip from the soil. Furthermore, beans are rich in the amino acid lysine which is essential for the effective digestion of the proteins found in corn. Together they provided the Salado with a protein rich, well balanced diet.

Agriculture, however, was always risky in this unpredictable climate. Prolonged drought or an unexpected flash flood could wipe out an entire season's harvest. Fortunately, nature provided alternatives in the more than 100 species of edible wild plants that are known to inhabit the Tonto Basin.

By late May, spring has departed to higher elevations, and summer is descending on the Salt River Valley. In the first searing heat of summer, the stately saguaro stages its yearly fashion show. The waxy, creamy-white blossoms which crown each arm of this giant cactus must have been a welcome sight to the Salado, signaling relief from the monotonous winter diet of dried foods. By late June or

early July, these blossoms mature into fruits that resemble small green cucumbers. When ripe, they burst open, revealing a deep red pulp filled with thousands of tiny black seeds. The sweet, succulent pulp is edible raw, or it can be boiled to make syrup, preserves, or wine. The oily seeds can be ground and used like butter. This first harvest of the year must have been an occasion for feasting, celebration, and ceremony.

Other cacti were also important food sources for the Salado. The dark red, pear-shaped fruits of the prickly pear were peeled and eaten raw or boiled down to syrup. The tender young pads can also be eaten raw or cooked as a green vegetable.

The mesquite tree provided the Salado with string beanlike pods that were ground into meal and made into cakes. The sap of the trees was used to make candy, to mend pottery, and as a black dye. The strong hardwood was made into tools and weapons and, of course, was used as firewood.

Yucca provided the Salado with both food and fiber. Buds, flowers and fruits are all edible. Indians preserved the large, bananalike fruits by roasting them and pressing the pulp into cakes which were dried in the desert sun. Its sharp-tipped leaves made excellent awls, and stringy leaf fibers were made into mats, baskets, sandals, string, rope, nets, and snares. Even the roots were useful, providing a soap and shampoo.

The agave provided a copious food supply. The leaves were chopped off, and the center of the living plant was slowly baked in an earth covered, stone-lined pit for at least 24 hours. This sweet, nutritious material was eaten like a giant artichoke and resembled the flavor of roasted yams or molasses.

These and countless other plants were used by the Salado to fulfill their needs. These Indians moved in harmony with the seasons and utilized the bounty of the desert.

SALADO CRAFT ARTS. Beautifully decorated Salado pottery and elaborate textiles illustrate a highly developed artistic sense. Sufficient free time to transform functional household goods into works of art is one indication of a thriving culture.

Pottery wheels were unknown to prehistoric Southwestern Indians. Instead, Salado women built up their pots with round rolls of clay which were coiled on each other. The potter then smoothed and shaped the walls of her vessel by placing one hand inside the pot and scraping the outside with a rounded sherd or gourd rind. The vessel could then be polished with a smooth stone, covered with a thin clay wash called a slip, and painted with elaborate designs. The vessel was fired over a bed of wood coals. The final color of the pot was largely determined by the amount of iron present in the clay.

Like other pueblo cultures, the Salado made plain red utility wares for everyday use. Their decorative wares consisted of three styles of beautifully painted polychromes which were reserved for ceremonial use and burial offerings.

Prehistoric pottery is named according to a two term classification system. The first name refers to a place where the type is known to occur; the second name refers to the color combination or surface treatment. Thus, Pinto polychrome is a pottery type found along Pinto Creek whose surface is painted in three colors. Pinto polychrome, Gila polychrome, and Tonto polychrome are all pottery types found in the Tonto Basin.

These Salado polychromes form one of the most popular pottery types ever produced in the Southwest and are often called the hallmark of the Salado tradition.

The textile artifacts excavated from the Tonto ruin form one of the finest collections of prehistoric fabrics in the Southwest. The Salado evolved a weaving

Tonto polychrome olla.

technology and artistry which rivaled that of any contemporary southwestern culture.

Cotton was grown in the irrigated fields near the river. When the cotton matured, the bolls were brought to the village and the fibers separated from the bolls and seeds. The fibers were spun into thread with a slender spindle stick which was weighted below the center with a flat disk called a whorl. Some of the skeins were dyed; others were left natural. There were various shades of brown, red, black, dark blue, dark blue-green, light blue and yellow.

Weaving tools have been discovered in male burials, suggesting that men did the weaving in pueblo cultures of the past, just as they do among the Hopi Indians today.

The diversity of weaves produced by these prehistoric Indians is astounding. Some were basic weaves used for large utilitarian items such as blankets and kilts. Others were technically complicated and produced elaborate designs. Only a few pieces of plaid have been found in the Southwest, one of which is a brown and white fragment found in the Tonto ruins.

The most popular decorative technique was weft-warp openwork. This cloth was basically a plain weave in which a design was created by wrapping horizontal weft threads around groups of vertical warp threads, pulling them apart to form small decorative holes. The finished product somewhat resembles drawnwork.

The finest example of Salado textile art in existence was found in the Tonto ruins. It is a man's shirt manufactured by an elaborate open work technique called twine-plaiting. this lacelike fabric is not woven. Instead, it is formed by twisting parallel pairs of threads around each other, then separating them to join with threads from adjoining pairs. Diamond and hexagonal-shaped holes are thus created which form airy decorative patterns in the cloth.

Textile collections from many prehistoric sites contain fragments of darned and patched cloth. This suggests that highly prized cotton textiles were carefully mended to last as long as possible. When a fabric was beyond repair it was torn into narrow strips which were used as weft threads for weaving heavy blankets.

These two major art forms, along with inlaid turquoise jewelry, beautifully woven baskets and cradleboards, finely crafted bone awls, brightly painted arrows and a host of other tools and implements for daily living reflect the ever-present human desire for creativity and artistic expression. These pieces of the past, found in archeological sites throughout the Tonto Basin, are helping archeologists to reconstruct the daily lives of the Salado people.

THE RUINS OF TONTO NATIONAL MONUMENT. The identity of the first white men to view the Tonto cliff dwellings will probably remain forever lost in time. Spanish conquistadors and robed friars first entered central Arizona in the 1540s and may have passed through the Tonto Basin, but sightings of the Tonto ruins were not recorded. Mountain men probably camped in the area in the 1820s and 30s, but again, no written records have survived.

The presence of the fierce Tonto Apache kept permanent settlers out of the basin until the mid 1870s, but by 1880 at least three large ranches had headquarters in the area. Early reports of the ruins suggested that cowboys from these ranches were their possible discoverers.

The famous Swiss-American archeologist Adolph Bandelier wrote the first professional report on the ruins following his visit to the Southwest in 1883. His detailed description of the ruins tells us that, "roofs, ceilings, doorways, hatchways are still mostly intact."

In 1906 the Bureau of Reclamation began construction of Roosevelt Dam. One of the greatest engineering feats of its day, the dam focused national attention on the Tonto Basin. This attention and increased public concern over the preservation of American antiquities caused President Theodore Roosevelt to create Tonto National Monument on December 19, 1907.

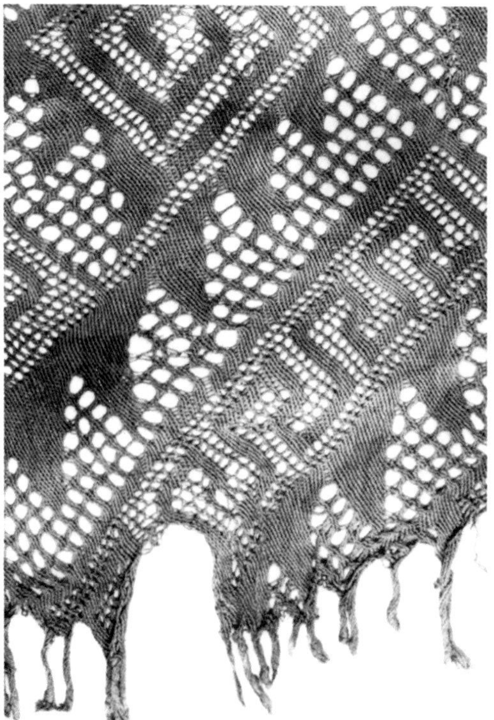

A fine example of Salado textile art.

The name "Tonto" is unrelated to the Salado Indians, who actually built the dwellings. Tonto is a Spanish word meaning foolish or stupid. The derivation of the name is somewhat obscure. One possible explanation is that Spanish explorers arriving in the Tonto Basin found a group of Apache who spoke a dialect not easily understood by neighboring Apache groups. Therefore, the Spanish called them the "Tonto Apache." The area inhabited by this band became known as the Tonto Basin, and the name spread from there.

When the 640 acre monument was created, it was placed under the jurisdiction of the U.S. National Forest Service. However, since the Forest Service had no money or personnel for the protection of the ruins, pothunters and vandals had free reign for many years. Floors were dug into and irreplaceable stratigraphic information was destroyed. Many valuable artifacts were lost.

With the completion of Roosevelt Dam in 1911, tourism became a major business in the basin. The construction of the Apache Trail made the area accessible to Phoenix area residents, and in 1911 the Southern Pacific Railroad opened a resort hotel on the north side of Roosevelt Dam. Of course, a stay in Roosevelt was not complete without a trip to the Tonto Ruins. Unfortunately, the ruins rapidly disintegrated under the unsupervised impact of both visitors and pot hunters. In order to preserve the ruins for its customers, the Southern Pacific Railroad obtained permission to erect a high fence around the two largest ruins. They also built a caretaker's house and employed an Apache Indian to act as a guide. This action was a great help in preserving the

site. The Government Reorganization Act of 1933 finally provided the ruins with the protection they deserved. This act placed the national monuments under the administration of the National Park Service. A temporary park ranger was soon assigned to oversee the site, and in 1937 the monument was expanded to its present size of 1,120 acres.

Although some sixty Salado sites have been located within the monument, many were unprotected from the elements and after 600 years of weathering only piles of boulders remain. The area is best known for its three major cliff dwellings, which are nestled in small caves high in the precipitous cliffs of Cave and Cholla canyons.

The Lower Ruin cave shelters a small structure of about twenty rooms. Sixteen ground floor rooms can still be traced; several of these had second stories. Archeologists have worked out the building sequence by studying wall junctions and sealed doorways. They believe the ruin was constructed in four separate building periods. Although accurate population estimates are difficult to make, the completed structure probably housed between forty and sixty people.

Three additional "basement" rooms were built outside and below the main cave. A ladder from the roof of these rooms led through a V-shaped notch that served as the front door of the dwelling. When the inhabitants wanted to close the door, they simply pulled up the ladder.

Although the Salado abandoned this pueblo nearly 600 years ago, there are still many signs of their daily lives. Smoke from cooking and heating fires blackened